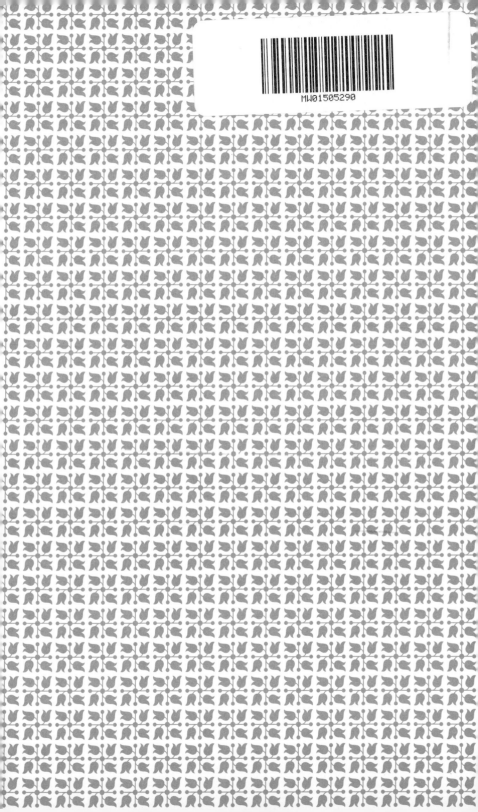

An Altar In Your Heart

Meditations on the Jesus Prayer

An Altar In Your Heart
Meditations on the Jesus Prayer

Robert B. Hibbs

20th Anniversary Edition

Foreword by Mary C. Earle
With Reflection Questions and Audio CD

No matter where we happen to be, by prayer we can set up an altar to God in our heart.

St. John Chrysostom

An Altar In Your Heart
Meditations on the Jesus Prayer

20th Anniversary Edition
Second Edition with Introduction, Reflection Questions, and audio CD
Copyright © 2018 by Robert B. Hibbs
(First Edition Copyright © 1998 by Robert B. Hibbs)

Foreword © 2018 Mary C. Earle
Reflection Questions © 2018 Mary C. Earle, Jennifer Garrett
Second Edition with Introduction, Reflection Questions, and audio CD
Illustrations courtesy of the artist © Luc Freymanc
All quotes from The Book of Common Prayer (Church Hymnal, 1979)
Author photo by Charles Parrish

Published by
New Beginnings, an imprint of
Material Media LLC
5150 Broadway #466
San Antonio, Texas 78209

ISBN: 978-0-9967535-9-3
Library of Congress Control Number: 2017945764

Printed in China

www.MaterialMedia.com
Material Media LLC
5150 Broadway #466
San Antonio, Texas 78209

An audio recording of the retreat is available to download from
MaterialMedia.com, and CDs are available from Stillpoint Media at
StillpointMedia.com or 800.241.2088.

Contents

Foreword

No doubt you have picked up this book because you have a desire to learn about the Jesus Prayer. Perhaps you also knew Robert Hibbs (Bob), who was an Episcopal priest and Bishop Suffragan of the Episcopal Diocese of West Texas. Or perhaps you attended the original retreat offered by Bob twenty years ago, and you have a desire to refresh your memory and renew your own devotional practice.

I first knew Bob Hibbs as a teacher. We met at the Episcopal Seminary of the Southwest in 1981, when my husband Doug and I moved to Austin. Bob was teaching ascetical theology at that time, and had a reputation on campus for delivering humorous, insightful stories and for having a very low opinion of the kind of spirituality that was all "pink bubbles and unicorns." Bob was a thoroughly incarnational Christian. He had no use for "Gnostic navel gazing" (see p. 66), the kind of "me and Jesus" spirituality that tends toward narcissistic concerns with no relation to the larger community or our neighbors. Following his Lord, Bob knew that we were called to follow the great commandment: You shall love the Lord your God with all your heart, and with all your soul, and with all your strength, and with all your mind; and your neighbor as yourself. (Luke 10:27, Deuteronomy 6:5, Leviticus 19:18)

Bob's teaching on the Jesus Prayer is grounded and clear. He lived and prayed within a regular discipline of praying the Daily Office (Morning Prayer, Noonday Prayer, Evening Prayer, Compline) and of participating in Holy Eucharist. His intellect led him to explore the historical languages of our faith, as well as Spanish and Tagalog. He savored words.

Yet Bob also knew—knew in his very bones—that words that do not come forth from deep silence often prove to be the verbal equivalent of fast food, with no real nutrition for heart, mind and soul.

Within these pages, the reader will encounter words that spring from the well of silence that framed Bob's life of prayer. He sought that essential balance between quiet and speech, rest and action. He lived long enough to know the truth of the Psalmist's proclamation: "For God alone my soul in silence waits; from him comes my salvation." (Ps. 62:1, Book of Common Prayer, p. 669) Those of us who knew Bob remember his stirring voice, which he used to good effect as a teacher, a preacher and a pastor. While many remember that voice in its fullest resonance, I remember it when Bob offered gentle, kind consolation in times of wrenching grief.

This 20th Anniversary Edition of *An Altar in Your Heart* is essentially the same as the original text. Some small changes in punctuation and wording have occurred. But the text itself is thoroughly, completely Bob Hibbs at his best as teacher and spiritual director. A man of many gifts, Bob was accomplished at weaving together insights from life, from Christian tradition, from theology, from The Book of Common Prayer. He was able to craft an integrated, invitational series of meditations on the Jesus Prayer because that was how he lived his life. Especially in his latter years, Bob sought to bring each aspect of his own rich and varied existence to the illumining grace of the Risen Christ. He learned to hold nothing back. He sought to offer all that he was, and all that he had, to the glory of God.

Being Bob, he could not do this in any saccharine way. It was fully embodied. His awareness of the mystical Body of Christ—enfleshed in human skin and bone, gut and sinew, muscle and brain and heart—led him to strongly insist on a communal, incarnational, open-hearted kind of spirituality. To his last days, he was obedient to praying the Daily Office of the Episcopal Church, even in the hospital. He never suggested practices or disciplines that encouraged self-focused piety with no regard for others.

Bob's ability to use the vernacular, especially the colloquial speech of his adopted home of Texas, led him to occasionally explain theology via the expressive language of that culture, both in English and in Spanish. He had a quirky sense of humor, in part because he knew life itself is quirky, unpredictable. One minute we are full of joy. The next we find ourselves wrenched by grief and distress. Within this text, you will find sentences that make you laugh, and sentences that make you think, reflect, ponder, wonder.

Because Bob's own life had been through the valley of the shadow of death more than once, he knew that the steadfast love of God was present in and through every circumstance we can imagine. He had come to know that the Christ "in whom all things hold together" (Colossians 1:17) held him together. Holds you together. Holds every single particle of the cosmos together. That steadfast love is creative, redemptive and sanctifying—love that will not let us go, and that is in all places and all times. Divine love is the ocean we swim in, the breath we breathe, the prayer that we offer.

Bob knew this in his heart, in his mind, in his gut. He had the gift of communicating that knowing through story and through image, through metaphor and remembrance. In this text, you will discover Bob's adroit ability to break open the text of the Jesus Prayer, and to begin to distribute its gifts. You will be given the opportunity to move at a gentle rhythm, to savor the prayer, and to attend to the movements of the Holy Spirit within your life and your world. You will find yourself invited to do more than read about the prayer. You will be led to pray.

As an Episcopalian, Bob participated actively in a tradition that knows that praying shapes believing, and praying shapes our lives. Bob had known from his childhood that regular worship takes us out of ourselves, into the objective faith of the 2,000-year-old tradition of Christianity. He delighted in the diversity of Sunday morning liturgies he encountered in his life as a bishop. He cherished the life of the tiny Church of the Ascension in Montell, Texas, as much as he cherished the life of the large Church of the Good Shepherd in Corpus Christi. Both offered the Holy Eucharist faithfully, not only for the gathered parishioners but for the life of the world.

I bring this up because in the background of this book abides Bob's life and experience as a celebrant of the Eucharist. He calls us to see our lives as bread for the world, as the Body of Christ, offered freely for our neighbors and for all of the creation. He directs us to remember that receiving the gifts of the sacramental life will always lead us back to seek and serve Christ in all others, loving our neighbors as ourselves.

By extension, Bob leads us to know that the Jesus Prayer will open our hearts and guide our wills so that we might be drawn to see that life is prayer, and prayer is life. Ultimately, this is what Bob received as truth. His habitual remembrance that we are living members of the Body of Christ shaped Bob's prayer and shaped his life.

Twenty years after the first edition of this book, we live in a culture beset by distraction and phenomenally shallow life. The various screens that commandeer our days tend not to be vehicles for deepening. Our attention spans, the neurologists tell us, have grown progressively shorter since Bob offered this retreat in 1998. As this fragmented, distressed version of the human psyche predominates, the Jesus Prayer offers us an alternative. As Bob points out, we come home to ourselves. Our truest selves. We come home to the fact of ever being in the loving presence of the Risen Christ, who holds our very cells in being. We come home to the awareness that there is no place where God is not. We come home to the stunning truth that we are never, ever alone, for the Risen Christ is the One in whom we live and move and have our being. Were that not the case, we simply would not exist.

Drawing on his regular use of The Book of Common Prayer, Bob ends each section with a prayer drawn from that resource. Each prayer is carefully chosen to illumine the insights he has offered about the Jesus Prayer. And, in a typically Hibbs-ian way, Bob intentionally juxtaposes the practice of the Jesus Prayer with the practice of praying with The Book of Common Prayer. He is telling us that these are good and lasting friends and that they will offer us steady companionship as we engage our own offering of prayer.

From time to time, Bob also refers to received tradition from the Christian faith. On pages 19–20 he offers the "Definition of the Union of the Divine and Human Natures in the Person of Christ." He gives the reader a direct link back to the Ecumenical Council of Chalcedon in 451 C.E. At that time, many opinions were held about whether Jesus was fully human, or fully divine. Conversations in drinking parlors centered around whether Jesus could possibly be fully human and fully divine. People came to blows over this. Consider that these spirited discussions took place some 450 years after Jesus was born. It took that long for this definition to reach its received form. (By comparison, 450 years ago the United States was not even in anyone's imagination. Exploration of North America was just beginning.)

Bob gave the reader this definition in part because he felt we needed to know it, and to receive it, and in part because it is foundational to the life of faith. Can we explain this? No. Can we understand it rationally? No. It is a profound and sacred mystery—a mystery that we journey into, letting go of fretful and frantic queries. This is the mystery of divine love embodied in Jesus who is the Christ—a mystery that we may rest in, a place where we may abide. As Bob remarks on p. 20, "This is God, who from the beginning before creation, in the tremendous loving dynamism and power of what that word 'God' means, was throbbing with love and energy." This is eternal, ever present, ever living, undying divine love embodied and known in Jesus who is the Christ.

Bob also notes that for some, the part of the Jesus Prayer that is traditionally "have mercy on me, a sinner," can cause difficulties. Bob, as a fine theologian and student of life, knew that while each person is created in the image and likeness of God, we are also born into families, societies and cultures that are fraught with patterns that are cruel and violent and mean-spirited. Bob knew how readily we could come to accept reductionist versions of who the human person is because those shallow, ridiculous, distorting versions are what the world of advertising gives us. Each of us is knit together in our mother's womb (Ps. 139:12). We are beautiful, sacred beings from the beginning. And yet, the web of relationships and culture into which we are born causes us to be blind to our own sacred nature, and to that sacredness of all others, and of the whole bright earth. This is the awareness that is behind the word "sinner" in the Jesus Prayer. It is not intended to make you feel like a worm. It is intended to awaken you to the "dullness of our blinded sight," and to stir your heart and soul toward living in mercy and grace.

Further, from the perspective of the Eastern Church, we are bound up in corporate structures of sin. For example, by myself I am neither fully responsible for climate change nor can my attempts to remedy that phenomenon alter the warming of the seas. That said, I am a participant in the communal lack of care for the creation, simply by being alive at this time. I am, in other words, a sinner with other sinners. For many of us in the Christian West, this dimension of our tradition has been forgotten. Beginning to grasp this aspect of the word "sinner," leads me to be ever mindful of the need for saving grace and healing mercy. I cannot heal the whole human family or myself, and I cannot heal the earth. Here we come to that oddest of Christian insights, spoken originally by St. Augustine of Hippo (5th century): "Without God, we cannot. Without us, God will not." We are inextricably bound up together, both in sin and in glory, in failure and in abundant life.

The Jesus Prayer will lead us both to renewed awareness of our glory, and abashed awakening to our participation in patterns of sinful behavior that hurt others, ourselves and the whole creation. This does not lead to being hopeless. Far from it. The prayer will guide us deeper and deeper into faith, hope and love. We are given eyes to see and ears to hear, so that we might name the goodness of God embodied in our everyday lives—in dogs and hummingbirds, in tamales and enchiladas, in friends and in strangers.

For, you see, this prayer, as Bob knew, will allow us to see the ongoing Incarnation of the beloved Christ right before our eyes. We will see anew, and begin to act in ways that honor the divine Presence in and through all aspects of our creation. This takes time.

It takes patience. It takes a willingness to know that God is working in and through the worst of circumstances, hallowing spaces defiled by misuse and violence. We will need to be humble enough to start over again and again, with lighthearted dedication and devotion.

Bob points us toward what has been known as "the beatific vision," a vision of God in Christ that is radiant with uncreated divine light, assuring us of ongoing steadfast love. As he points out repeatedly, the Jesus Prayer is an option. Not all who read this book will be led to pray in this particular way. And that is fine. Others will discover, or encounter again, the practice of allowing the mind to descend to the heart, thereby remembering the Holy One who has created all that is, and allowing that Beloved to infuse our lives with confidence in a divine Presence that delights in us and calls us friends.

Lord Jesus Christ, Son of God,
Have mercy on me, a sinner. Amen.

The Rev. Mary C. Earle
Ordinary Time, June 2017

Acknowledgements

When Jenny and Charles Garrett of Stillpoint Media first broached the idea of turning the tapes of my retreat addresses on the Jesus Prayer into a small book, I was frankly incredulous. Their confidence and continuing kindly persuasion form the genesis of this work, and I am deeply appreciative.

It is no small feat to turn the idiosyncrasies of my spoken word into written form. I know, because I have tried unsuccessfully on several occasions. Marjorie George, Communications Officer of the Diocese of West Texas, has given more time than I can think of without embarrassment to this task, and her considerable skill has captured the style and cadence of the spoken original. By George, and only by George, this transcription happened. I am deeply grateful.

Nancy Joane Hibbs, my wife and friend of 40 years, is, under God, the foundation of any good thing I may do.

+Bob Hibbs
Epiphanytide, 1998

Lord Jesus Christ, Son of God,
Have mercy on me, a sinner. Amen.

Introduction

The material in this little book was first presented during a retreat held on the Texas Gulf Coast in 1995. It was a wonderful time of long walks on the beach, listening to waves lap the shore, and watching seagulls retrieve their dinner from the blue waters of the Gulf of Mexico. It was particularly appropriate because the Jesus Prayer itself is a kind of retreat—a little spot of respite from the frantic pace of our late twentieth century.

I invite you to read this material in the posture of a retreat, to amble through it at a leisurely pace, pausing—perhaps for a day or several days—to reflect upon it as you make your way through it.

And I invite you to enter into a kind of quiet as you allow the material to engage you.

Now, there are two kinds of quiet, and they're not unrelated. The first is what some people call inner quiet. Years ago, I went to seminary in New York City, and nobody's ever thought that New York City was a quiet place. But even in the midst of all that urban din, I learned I could be quiet on the inside. I remember once studying for a theology exam in Grand Central Station.

So allow yourself the gift of inner quiet while you read; block out the things of the world and of your life that pull on you for attention. Just let them go for a while; they'll still be there when you get back to them. You'll find that the Jesus Prayer itself is a way to establish inner quiet.

There is also an outer quiet, and that is basically a matter of not talking. I invite you to help yourself to generous intervals of not talking after each period of reading this material. Take your own long walk on the beach, or in the woods, or through the meadow —even if metaphorically—to digest and mull over for a while what you have read.

A second thing to bear in mind as you read is that your thoughts, your reflections, whatever comes to you through the work of the Holy Spirit is every bit as valid and important as anything in the reading. God is the one who is going to do whatever is going to get done. Allow him to speak to you in a very private and personal way through these pages. But don't even work at that too hard; sometimes, you know, prayer is not a matter of saying or doing— it's a matter of being.

The Rt. Rev. Bob Hibbs
Epiphanytide, 1998

Chapter One

ORIGINS

It will help us, I think, as we take apart the Jesus Prayer, to first look at it as a whole.

The Jesus Prayer is something that the saints have known for years and years as a venerable method of not just prayer but of being with God, of living in the presence of God. It is one of the primary devotional motifs in Orthodox Christianity—found centuries ago in the Russian Church and the Greek Church, among others.

The roots of the prayer go right back to the New Testament itself where St. Paul talks about "praying without ceasing" and where we read that no one can say that Jesus is Lord except by the inspiration of the Holy Spirit.

The elements of the Jesus Prayer can be found in the church of the first apostles; but as a developed devotional system, it was during the third and fourth centuries that the prayer began to emerge as a body of doctrine, a body of teaching.

But the Jesus Prayer is not a panacea. It won't cure dandruff, and it won't "magic away" reality. And it's not for everyone. It may occupy a place in your life that is different from the place it occupies in my life. At times it has been a very important part of my spiritual discipleship, and other times it has sort of been in the background. Some people find it becomes almost the centerpiece of their spiritual life; for other people, it might be just one arrow they have in their devotional quiver.

Or the Jesus Prayer may not be for you at all; in that case, pass this book on to someone else and continue your own search for ways of touching God and allowing him to touch you that excite your mind and stroke your heart.

So, this is the Jesus Prayer:

Lord Jesus Christ, Son of God, have mercy on me, a sinner.

That is the basic form. There are variants to that text; some forms don't include "a sinner, " so that it is just:

Lord Jesus Christ, Son of God, have mercy on me.

In its most attenuated form, when it gets all the way down to its roots, it can simply consist of the loving repetition of the holy name of Jesus.

It is a very simple prayer, bringing together in one short sentence, one utterance, two essential moments of Christian devotion: adoration and penitence.

The easiest way to say what's contained in the Jesus Prayer is this: it's Good Friday, and it's Easter.

Lord Jesus Christ, Son of God—Easter; have mercy on me, a sinner—Good Friday.

It's always Easter, and it's always Good Friday. You can't have one without the other.

A second thing about the Jesus Prayer is that it's an intensely Christological prayer. That's a 50-cent word theologians use to say that it's intensely focused on Jesus. As we unpack these Christological dimensions, we'll find that the prayer concentrates on both the human person of the incarnate Lord and on his divinity.

When we consider first the Incarnation—God taking human form—we have to remember that Christianity is not a gaseous religion: it's not airy, fairy, floaty. Christianity has guts to it; it has armpits, it's got cracked toenails. It's got body parts, and the Jesus Prayer grabs us with the "enfleshedness" of God's love and of our own "enfleshedness." There are many, many patterns of spirituality, but every authentic Christian pattern of spirituality is rooted and grounded in the Incarnation. I would go so far as to say that any pattern of spirituality that is not rooted in the Incarnation is, to that extent, less than fully Christian.

The richness of the Jesus Prayer is that it also concentrates on the divinity of Jesus. That's why it really is a very orthodox, in every sense of the word, devotion. It's a way of praying our faith in the Incarnation and, at the same time, bowing to the divine.

And yet, the Jesus Prayer is a prayer of utmost simplicity. You really don't need a lot of equipment to "do" it. Sometimes in the morning as I do my walking, I'll use my prayer beads to run through the prayer, but I also use my fingers a lot; I've got ten of them, I can go on forever.

(Even to this day, when a man or a woman becomes a monk or a nun in any one of the Orthodox churches, he or she is given a prayer rope which is a primary tool for developing this unceasing prayer that is such an important part of the religious life in the Orthodox church. The prayer rope is, in fact, much older than the rosary in the Western Church. As an element to move through your fingers as you pray through the Jesus Prayer, the use of a prayer rope goes back to the very beginning of Christian devotion. You might want to try one.)

Or I can sit in a doctor's office and use each person waiting there as a bead. I just drift around the room.

I once read that Cardinal Mindzenty, who was Primate of the Hungarian Church during the horrible time of the Cold War, was arrested and spent years in solitary confinement. When he got out, he was asked, "How did you survive?" And the answer was, "Lord Jesus Christ, Son of God, have mercy on me, a sinner."

One of my teachers at the Pontifical Institute, a Dominican priest in Toronto, Canada, was Isadore Eschmann. Father Eschmann was one of those Roman Catholics in Germany during the thirties who refused to go along with Adolf Hitler. They put Father Eschmann through some horrible exercises. What kept him going? He didn't need a lot of equipment; he didn't need any books: Lord Jesus Christ, Son of God, have mercy on me, a sinner.

Almighty and eternal God, so draw our hearts to you, so guide our minds, so fill our imaginations, so control our wills that we may be wholly yours, utterly dedicated to you, and then use us, we pray, as you will, and always to your glory and the welfare of your people. Through our Lord and Savior Jesus Christ, Amen. (Book of Common Prayer, 1979, p. 832-833)

**Lord Jesus Christ, Son of God,
Have mercy on me, a sinner. Amen.**

Personal Reflection

As you begin your experience of the Jesus Prayer, how might you find space for this prayer in your daily life?

Chapter Two

LORD JESUS CHRIST, SON OF GOD

One of the great journals of Christendom is *Cistercian Studies*, published by the Cistercian Fathers, an order in the Roman Catholic church. It was an article that appeared in the journal some time ago that evoked my own interest in the Jesus Prayer, and much of what I know comes from that article. So let's examine the Jesus Prayer a little bit.

The first word in the Jesus Prayer is "Lord." How many times in the course of a week, a day, do we use the word "Lord" in our praying?

Lord Jesus Christ.
Lord Jesus.
Lord, help me.
Lord, Lord, Lord.

It's a remarkable word, Lord. In the Greek, it's *Kyrie*, the vocative form, the address form of the word *Kyrios*.

In all likelihood, prior to the resurrection nobody ever called Jesus, "Lord." First of all, they wouldn't have called him "Lord" because they didn't use Greek in conversation. They would have spoken Aramaic, maybe occasionally Hebrew.

So they wouldn't have called Jesus "*Kyrie.*" They may have called him "Rabbi"—my teacher.

It was after the resurrection and after the empowering of the church by the Holy Spirit, and most especially after the influx of those non-Jewish people into the church, that this expression—*Kyrie, Kyrie,*

Lord, Lord—would have become part of the common property of the prayer language. Lord is one of the titles of divinity, used even by the pagans in antiquity. They would have talked about *Kyrios Apollos*—Lord Apollo. Or *Kyrios* Dionysius, or *Kyrios* Zeus—Lord Dionysius, Lord Zeus.

But then, in the fullness of time, by his cross and passion, by his glorious resurrection and ascension, and by the coming of the Holy Spirit, Jesus was revealed as the one true Lord.

Thomas, in the upper room, was very close. After that second resurrection appearance in the upper room, it was Thomas who insisted, "Unless I can put my fingers into the wound, unless I can put my hand into the side, I will not, I cannot." And so Jesus, there in that upper room, said, "Thomas, don't be such a schnook, come here, do it." So Thomas did, and then he cried out, in Greek, *"Ho Kyrios mou"*— my Lord—and, *"Ho theos mou"*—and my God. There it is: Lord, Lord.

You see, we need to be very careful we don't get hornswoggled into the cult of sweet Jesus, mild Jesus, wimpy Jesus. We need to not do that, simply because it's not what the New Testament says about him. It's not what the primitive church knew about him. They knew him as king, as royalty, as divinity, as Lord.

His name, as a child, was probably Jehoshua— Joshua. We've anglicized it to Jesus.

Jehoshua means "Yahweh is my salvation, Yahweh is my savior."

One reason why Jewish males wear yarmulkes is that any form of the divine name "Yahweh" is so sacred, so holy, that you would not presume to have it uttered without the reverence of a covered head.

I grew up in an Anglican family of strict obser-vance in Philadelphia, and as a child, I remember that whenever you said the name of Jesus, you'd bow your head. It's so holy, you'd just bow your head. The ladies used to curtsy whenever they heard the name, Jesus. That's the old, strict observance.

Yahweh is my salvation; Yahweh is my savior. That's really what the name Jesus means: Savior. It's a name that describes who he is.

Our medieval sisters and brothers in the faith had a wonderful prayer. It was: *Jesus esto mihi Jesus*—Jesus be to me a Jesus. Jesus be to me a savior. Savior be to me a savior. Savior be to me a Jesus. It all just sort of flows together. Lord, Jesus. You see it growing?

The second part of the title is Christ—Jesus, the Christ. Christ is the direct Greek translation of the Hebrew word "Messiah." When we say Jesus Christ, we're really saying Jesus, the Messiah. *Jesus Christos,* or as it regularly appears in the New Testament: *Jesus ho Christos,* Jesus, the Christ, Jesus the Messiah. It's a title. If Lord is the title of divinity, Christos is the title of his anointedness.

Do you remember how kings were chosen in ancient history? Samuel was an example of it. There was a terrible conflict in the ancient community of our Jewish ancestors—would they have a king or would they not? Some people absolutely demanded that God give them a king, and other people thought they dared not have a king because the only King to have was Yahweh. Finally, the word of the Lord came to Samuel, and he took a vial of oil and poured it out over the head of Saul. It was in that anointing that the Holy Spirit came, the *Ruach Elohim*, the Spirit of God which came upon Saul and he became King of Israel. It was the anointing with the oil that was the occasion, and the word used for what happened to Saul was he became *mashiach*, he became a messiah. He became a christ. And ever after all of the kings—Saul, Solomon, and even Solomon's no-good son, Rehoboam—were all anointed, they were all *mashiach*.

Even after the split, when one of the two kingdoms went to the north and one to the south and the whole story became a pitiful, sad story of a decline in faith and a decline in obedience and of exile and captivity, even those insignificant little kings were *mashiach*—they were anointed.

Then in the fullness of time, there came One who did not speak the words about God, but who was himself the Word made flesh. At his baptism in the river Jordan, the Spirit came upon him. It was the outpouring of the Spirit of the living God, that Spirit which brooded in the beginning of all time. And he was *mashiach* and King, anointed. Lord Jesus Christ, anointed Son of God. The Council of Chalcedon, in 451 A. D., put it this way:

> Therefore, following the holy fathers, we all with one accord teach men to acknowledge one and the same Son, our Lord Jesus Christ, at once complete in Godhead and complete in manhood, truly God and truly man, consisting also of a reasonable soul and body; of one substance with the Father as regards his Godhead, and at the same time of one substance with us as regards his manhood; like us in all respects, apart from sin; as regards his Godhead, begotten of the Father before the ages, but yet as regards his manhood begotten, for us men and for our salvation, of Mary the Virgin, the God-bearer; one and the same Christ, Son, Lord, Only-begotten, recognized in two natures, without confusion, without change, without division, without separation; the distinction of natures being in no way annulled by the union, but rather the characteristics of each nature being preserved and coming together to form one person and subsistence, not as parted or separated into two persons, but one and the same Son and Only-begotten God

the Word, Lord Jesus Christ; even as the prophets from earliest times spoke of him, and our Lord Jesus Christ himself taught us, and the creed of the Fathers has handed down to us. (BCP, 1979, p. 864)

This is God, who from the beginning before creation, in the tremendous loving dynamism and power of what that word "God" means, was throbbing with love and energy. What proceeds from him is the Eternal Word of God, the divine self-knowledge, that thing, that being, which shares all of God's creative power and energy and beauty and majesty and dominion. The Word of God. What God knows about God. That's the son, S-O-N. That's the Son of God in his uncreated, consubstantial, coeternal splendor. All of those big, heavy words.

And then, in the fullness of time, for love of us— and love of all of us in every time and every place getting very, very small and helpless, and in a time and in a place and in a manger becoming one with us. Son of God—very, very, very big and very, very, very small.

Lord Jesus Christ, Son of God.

That's the ecstasy of the Jesus Prayer.

It's the Easter part; it's the Alleluia part. And what a universe of theology, what a universe of experience is compressed into that. You see, it's really a kind of embryonic creed. It has to do with creation; it has to do with incarnation; it has to do with resurrection. All that the church has been doing, and really all that the church will ever do, is just kind of meditate and reflect, and meditate and reflect, and meditate and reflect the Lord Jesus Christ as Son of God.

Direct us, O Lord, in all our doings with your most gracious favor, and further us with your continual help; that in all our works begun, continued, and ended in you, we may glorify your holy Name, and finally, by your mercy, obtain everlasting life; through Jesus Christ our Lord. Amen. (BCP, 1979, p. 832)

Lord Jesus Christ, Son of God,
Have mercy on me, a sinner. Amen.

Personal Reflection

How does the Jesus Prayer aid your awareness of what Bob Hibbs calls "the Easter part"?

As that awareness has grown and shifted, how has that created and renewed your own attitudes and actions?

Chapter Three

HAVE MERCY ON ME, A SINNER

I get offended by some of the popular theology, which is all over the place, the theology of paperback books that talks about God, "my cosmic buddy."

Sure, there's a sense in which I do need God as my companion. But God is not just the manager of the celestial country club. And when ultimately I see God, I'm not going to walk up and say, "Good morning, God, it's a pleasure to meet you, I am profoundly honored."

No. I like the ancient words of the Eucharist better: "Therefore with angels and archangels and with all the company of heaven…" Whenever we say that you can see the whole church bowing down in profound adoration as it says, "Holy, Holy, Holy, Lord God."

The more I know who God is, and I never, never have perfect knowledge, and then the more I know who I am, the more I know what I want from God: mercy, patience, love.

I have a friend who is an Episcopal priest and about an umpteenth generation Texan, who had an aunt named Lonnie. Apparently, she was the terror of the family—one of these really poisonous, passive-aggressive people who just broke other people wherever she went. You know the kind: "If you love me, you will…" All of the family belonged to the Umbadumblian Church, except for this weird guy who turned out to be a priest in a church that sounded like Pepsi-Cola spelled sideways. Anyway, Aunt Lonnie died, and so it seemed only appropriate to have the priest say something. So there they all were at this neat little cemetery by the riverside, and they sang "Amazing Grace" and all that good stuff. Then my friend got up and he stood by the hole where Aunt Lonnie's body was and he said, "If God is a God of justice only, Aunt Lonnie is in Hell right now."

And that's the truth. But it's not just the truth for Aunt Lonnie; it's the truth for all of us. If God is a God of justice only, there is no good news; there's nothing. What we need is mercy. We absolutely need it; without it, we cannot stand. Without it, we cannot live.

The beautiful thing is that when we ask God for mercy, we are not pleading with God to give us something he is reluctant to give. It is God's joy and God's delight, the essence of who he is, to give us what we plead for. And so the cry of the Jesus prayer is not a cry for "Oh, I hope he will do it," but "Oh, he does it, over and over and over again." It is the mercy of God, the grace of God, and his lovely transubstantiating power that takes the bread and wine of my life, and of all of our lives, and blesses it and breaks it and recreates it to make it more than it could ever, ever, ever be. All of that is grace and all of that is mercy. And it's the stream we swim in. "Have mercy" is not just a heart-rending petition; it's an outburst of our experience. We cry to the God of mercy for mercy. It's our breath; it's our life, it's our water, it's our air. Have mercy on me. Who is "me"?

Some of us have a horrible time with "me." We fly on a kind of a trapeze between two selves. One is god-like, a me that is the product of illusion and delusion, an arrogant me, a me who is powerful, a me who is self-sufficient, a me who is grandiose, a me who is self-will run riot, a me who will trample over people I love and devour them and consume them. A me who wants what I want when I want it, a me who is pathological and pathogenic. A me who is sick as hell.

If that me is the grandiose phony, the other me is the grandiose negative phony.

"I'm nothing; I'm a worm, oh God, oh God," this one goes. And we sway and we stagger back and forth between the two.

In the Jesus Prayer, we talk about me, the real me, the creature me, the one who is not absolute in any way. The one who is limited, the one who is real, the one who can love, but who needs help to love; the one who can know, but who needs help to know; the one who can will and does will in a limited, created way; but the one who needs help to will the good and avoid the evil. But above all, the me who is at every moment loved by God, who is the apple of God's eye. Who, when I walk through the valley of the shadow of death, will be with me and in me and for me.

Be merciful, have mercy upon the real me. Because I am not a worm, but a sinner. I am broken; I'm busted.

There's a lot of American religion that is kind of turning into a sort of religious cheerleading. And it works up to a point. I get inspired, I get the warm fuzzies of religious enthusiasm. I go to retreats and come away shouting, "Excelsior!"

The difficulty is if I just trust me, there is no god I will not blaspheme, no truth I will not dishonor, and no good I will not betray. And I know that, and I cannot pull myself up by my own bootstraps. I'm not the little engine that thought it could. I need help.

Jesus said to his disciples, and that includes us, "Without me, you can do nothing." I need Jesus—I need God's grace—I need the Father and the Son and the Holy Spirit—not as a pious option, not as a second mile of religious devotion. I need help to be the real me. That's what it means to be a sinner. I just need help. And God says, " I know you do. And good you know it. You need it and I'll do it."

Wonderful prayer, theologically rich, psychologically profound: Lord Jesus Christ, Son of God, be merciful to me, a sinner.

Lord, make us instruments of your peace. Where there is hatred, let us sow love. Where there is injury, pardon. Where there is discord, union. Where there is doubt, faith. Where there is despair, hope. Where there is

darkness, light. Where there is sadness, joy. Grant that
we may not so much seek to be consoled as to console;
to be understood as to understand; to be loved as to love.
For it is in giving that we receive; it is in pardoning that
we are pardoned; and it is in dying that we are born to
eternal life. (BCP, 1979, p. 833)

**Lord Jesus Christ, Son of God,
Have mercy on me, a sinner. Amen.**

Personal Reflection

*How have you known Divine Mercy in your life? How
have you extended mercy to others?*

Chapter Four

MAKING IT YOURS:
Working with the
Jesus Prayer

The first thing you have to do if you're going to use the Jesus Prayer is at some point say, "I will try it." There has to be that assent of the will. You know what it is, you're finding out a little bit about it and so it's not just an ineffable mystery, it's a way to pray, and you have to say, "I will try it."

There's another equally good response and that is, "I will not try it."

Either way is good. The Jesus Prayer is not the only way to salvation. It's not the only way to sanctity. It's a possibility; it's a good possibility, but it may not feel right for you.

I know for myself, the first time I heard about it I was fascinated by it, but it was kind of a little bit spooky, a little too far out, and I think I really wasn't ready. So I had to say, "Thanks, but no thanks." And that may be the case for you. What we need to avoid, all of us need to avoid, is spiritual dilettantism: the mentality of Jesus Prayer one week and spiritual growth through drinking carrot juice the next. I don't know any serious spiritual writer or spiritual teacher who recommends that.

One of my good friends is St. Benedict, whose Rule is the basis of a whole household of spirituality. In his Rule, Benedict talks about detestable monks, which is pretty strong. They even have a kind of ugly name, they are the *gyrovagues*. Like a gyroscope that is running down, they stumble and stagger around, going from one monastery and spiritual director to the next. In our own day, there's a lot of that. There are people, for instance, who become addicted to retreating—the only time they ever come alive is when they go on a retreat and get turned on by whatever or whoever is the star of that particular show for that particular weekend.

That's spiritually unhealthy. It's a "feel-good-ism." It's searching for the tingle, and it's selfish. It becomes a kind of fascination with religious feelings. Ultimately, all spirituality is tested not by whether it feels good, but to what extent it impels us into apostolic action, to what extent it forces us to come to grips with the imperative to be Christ in the environment in which we find ourselves.

We're always in danger, especially if we think we are spiritually superior, of becoming cesspools of grace. It just flows in, and it flows in, and it flows in, and it never flows out. We're always sort of sucking it up, but we never, never get to being Christ in the environment.

The Al-Anon people have a phrase—"Try 90 meetings in 90 days, and if that doesn't work, we'll refund your misery." I like that. If you really want to find out something about the Jesus Prayer, take off a nice chunk of time, like 90 days, and say, "For the next three months, I'm going to really see if this is for me." Try it, and grow with it. Check in with your spiritual director or with your parish priest and if he or she is in favor, give it the old college try.

I once said to a group of people that I'm not really interested in books that were written after the invention of printing. What I meant was there is a problem related to our easy access to unlimited numbers of religious books. The Rev. Dr. Von Schlugenbugen makes a pronouncement and everybody goes off on a tangent, and you read and you read. We get into the mode of any spiritual thrill that you can thrill, I can thrill better.

Be careful of that. It can result in a kind of super-ficiality. Every one of us sooner or later is going to have to go through the real thing. For sure. There's death, and there's dying, and there's sin, and there's tough stuff out there. And that's when some of that light stuff that floats on the surface will betray you. It's like a lifejacket that's lost its buoyancy. Real spirituality is very valuable. As you begin to work with the Jesus Prayer, be certain you're approaching it with some solid intention: "I will try it," or, equally good, "It's interesting, but it's not for me." And that's fine.

The Jesus Prayer in the beginning really is an oral prayer. You have to say the words aloud. I encourage you to find some place where you can do that with some degree of abandon. Say it with all of your muscles, with your fingernails, and your toenails, and your belly button. To just reduce the prayer to a kind of a thinky, thoughty kind of thing neglects the lovely thing that God has created. So, get out there and stride along. And when nobody's looking— because, after all, we are all kind of uptight—just do it. You'll be fine.

Now a second element, in the beginning, is deliberate acts of the will that fix the attention on the prayer. You could observe, "Well, it's now 4:25, and for the next five minutes, I'm going to do it." Just be kind of tough. If we wait around until we're inspired to pray, the chances are real good that we're going to be cheapskate prayers. I don't know about you, but I don't get up in the morning and throw open the window and shout, "Alleluia." On Sunday mornings I don't think, "Oh, blessed be thou, Lord God, king of the universe, now I get to go to church." No, no, no. It doesn't work like that. It's morning and I'm a responsible human being, I've been ordained to do certain things, and it's got nothing to do with how I feel about it. It is my bounden duty as a Christian to do x and y and z, my bounden duty as a priest to do x and y and z. So womanfully or manfully I pledge to do five minutes of the Jesus Prayer. In the tradition of the Jesus Prayer, quantity is also important in the beginning.

Are you old enough to have learned to drive in a conventional shift car with a clutch? Aren't you glad you learned to do that? Once you got the hang of it, it was really neat. But do you remember learning to do it? Oh boy, if there ever was an exercise in patting your head and rubbing your tummy at the same time. You had to think your way—now I will depress the clutch, and now pull it down here, then let out the clutch and give it the gas and it goes, and put in the clutch… And it was awful, just awful. You had to do it many, many times until it became second nature. Eventually, you got so good you could downshift to slow the car down. And then you could stop it and hold it on a steep hill. Remember all that? The only way you developed that facility is because you'd done it enough times. Even now, sometimes, I really like it when the rental car is a stick shift.

That's the way it is with the Jesus Prayer. You practice, you do it without thinking.

Or use your breathing: on the inhale say, "Lord Jesus Christ, Son of God," and on the exhale, "Have mercy on me, a sinner."

In all of it, relax. Spirituality, good spirituality, healthy spirituality usually has a little element of playfulness. If you find yourself getting terribly white knuckled, ease up. If you find yourself hyperventilating, quit. Play a little. Enjoy.

When you first begin to use the Jesus Prayer, you're going to be distracted. You just cannot help but be distracted. Get ready for it. You'll start to pray then find yourself thinking about everything. Or you'll begin to worry about what's going to happen next week, and what's going to happen next month. Always that static goes on. Always, always.

I want to make a suggestion about distraction in prayer in general, and distraction in prayer with the Jesus Prayer. Don't be impatient with yourself. If you find yourself saying, "Oh, I did it again," stop all that. Of course, you did it again. It doesn't mean you're wicked and it doesn't mean you're bad, it just means that you're human. Gently, gently, when you find yourself distracted in prayer, gently turn away from the distraction. Gently. One of the great spiritual writers says—and this is kind of ponderous, but it's kind of lovely—that when you find yourself distracted from your prayer, say, "I have turned aside from my prayer. I will return to my prayer."

Now my final statement is—and this is a quote from one of those old, bearded Russian fathers— "The attentive repetition of the prayer often proves a hard and exhausting task, calling for humble persistence." I don't know anybody who's into the Jesus Prayer who hasn't gone through humble persistence. Stick to it, humbly, persistently, gently, not arrogantly.

So, it's oral prayer, and it requires deliberate acts of the will: "I'm going to do it, I'm going to do it for the next five minutes, for the next ten minutes. And I'm going to do it over and over and over again," and with humble persistence.

Then the next step is that in time the prayer becomes inward. It's going to take you a while to get to step two, but there are some indicators that let you know when this is happening. The oral part, the moving of the lips and the tongue, becomes less important. You can still do it, and you'll want to do it, but the prayer is going even when you're not doing that. It doesn't require the mechanics of your lips.

The concentration of the attention becomes easier. Once my wife said to me, "Bob, quit praying the Jesus Prayer while you're driving, because you're starting to wander off the road." She was right.

Thirdly, and this is very significant, the prayer gradually acquires a rhythm of its own. Not always the same rhythm, but it comes. In the morning when I'm walking, without my knowing it I'll begin to realize that the prayer is just bouncing along with the cadence of my body's movement. It develops this rhythm. It may begin to relate to the way I'm breathing, or it may pick up the rhythm of my heartbeat.

Eventually, the prayer enters the heart. The rhythm is identified more and more closely with the movement of the heart until it becomes unceasing. It just goes on and on and on and it never stops. It has entered the heart, and as long as the heart is beating, the heart is praying the Jesus Prayer. And what was originally something that required painful and strenuous effort is now an inexhaustible source of peace and joy.

But you can't worry about "attaining" the third stage. It's God's gift; it will come. Be persistent in stage one and stage two and sooner or later in time or eternity, it will be all right. Just don't worry about it. The overwhelming majority of people who practice the Jesus Prayer are in the first and second stage. There's an old Baptist hymn that says, "Take time to be holy." Holiness requires taking time. There is no instant holiness. It takes time. Lots of prayer, lots of meditations, lots of confessions, lots of communions—it takes time. It's part of our world's problem with sanctity—we live in a world where you just add water and you've got soup, you've got coffee. There's no mystical, magical hoo-ha powder you can put into a cup and add water and stir and you drink it and it will make you holy. It won't work. So, don't worry about the third stage—it's God's gift. Take time. A lifetime.

Here's some advice: avoid worrying about concepts and images. When I was in seminary, we had a visiting English bishop come and give us a course in meditating. He was using a gospel story which occurred in a boat, and he said, "Picture Jesus in a boat." Well, most of my life I have had lousy vision, so visual imaging is not my long suit, and I could no more picture Jesus in a boat than I could fly by flapping my ears.

After class, I went to the bishop and I said, "Bishop, I'm a goner, because I cannot picture Jesus in a boat." And he laughed at me because I was such an earnest little guy. Then he said, "Well, what can you do? Does the sense of the presence of God mean anything to you?" And I said, "Well, yes, sure. One night when I was very young, while Mama and I were doing the 'Now I lay me down to sleep,' and the 'God blesses,' I had this feeling that there was someone else in the room with us. So after Mama had left the room, I climbed out of bed and got down on my knees and did my prayers again to see if the someone was still there, and he was. And that was the beginning of something."

"Well," said the bishop, "never mind all this picture stuff. Just be in the presence."

The Jesus Prayer is about contemplation, about being in the presence of God.

My wife and I dated for a long time before getting married. I remember that when we began to date, we had so much to talk about. Talk, talk, talk, talk. And we had so much in common. We were very busy together. But eventually, we were content to just be with each other. We had a favorite pizzeria, and we'd go there and just hold hands across the pizza.

A lot of prayer is busyness. You have these lists, you have rules of life, you say Morning Prayer and Evening Prayer and Wednesday nights and all of that.

The Jesus Prayer is not so much being busy as it is being in a mutual relationship of loving regard between you and Jesus. Just hold hands across the pizza.

But the Jesus Prayer also presupposes some things. It presupposes living in grace as a vital, living member of the body of Christ. It presupposes regular communion, regular confessions, other prayers. It presupposes singing in the choir, working on the altar guild, being regular at church, all of that stuff. The Jesus Prayer is not the prayer of a spiritual lone ranger; it's the prayer of somebody who is deeply imbedded in the life of grace, in the risen life of Christ.

Assist us mercifully, O Lord, in these our supplications and prayers, and dispose the way of your servants toward the attainment of everlasting salvation; that, among all the changes and chances of this mortal life, they may ever be defended by your gracious and ready help; through Jesus Christ our Lord. Amen. (BCP, 1979, p. 832)

Lord Jesus Christ, Son of God,
Have mercy on me, a sinner. Amen.

Personal Reflection

What deliberate, intentional discipline do you hope to embrace for praying the Jesus Prayer?

How does this prayer help you become aware of the presence of God, in all places and at all times?

Chapter Five

FOCUSING THE JESUS PRAYER

One of the basic concepts about the Jesus Prayer that is difficult—not because it's really difficult, but because it's new and unusual—is the idea of the prayer in the heart.

The Eastern Orthodox have been at it for 2000 years now, but for Westerners, it's harder to comprehend, and it begins with asking, "Where is Jesus?" Right away you will say, "everywhere," or, "he's in heaven." But both of those answers have residual problems. If you say "everywhere," that is too diffuse. We're not everywhere; we're right here. How do we get him here? I have the same problem with Jesus being located in heaven.

I think we have to recognize that one of the things that make Christianity different from the other religions is its "physicalness," its "fleshiness," its "stuffness." It comes to us out of the Jewish womb from which we were born. As soon as we say with St. John, "In the beginning was the Word, and the Word was God, and all things were made by him and without him was not anything made that was made…and the Word became flesh and dwelt among us." As soon as we've said that, we've said something that's uniquely Christian. And we've said something that means that all of our thinking about spirituality has to be incarnational spirituality, has to be fleshly spirituality, has to be sacramental spirituality, and we've got to be able to say something about where Jesus is in terms of other than in heaven.

Jesus is in all created things; he is in other people, other human beings, however defaced by sin. He's in us; he's in me.

Jesus is the creative word of God by whom all things were made. Do you remember the Genesis story? The word of God that comes roaring forth and says, "Let there be ... " and there is. There is not a thing in the room where you sit right now—nothing—that is not sustained in being by the word of God. The chair that's supporting your weight is a creature. It's a lovely creature. It's being sustained in being right this moment. Physics teaches us that there's tremendous energy and power in the chair that's holding you up. There is a tremendous dynamism. It's not just a static lump of stuff. My goodness, there's enough stuff in your chair to blow up six worlds. It's throbbing with being. And the reason it's throbbing with being is that the Creative Word is sustaining it in being. Now, do you know what's going to happen to you if God stops being present in the chair you're sitting on? You're going to fall on your fanny.

Now, for a moment, focus your attention—your prayer, if you will, the presence of the Word of God, the Word made flesh in Jesus—on some created thing. Pick anything—your shoelace, your cross, your pencil, your chair. Just grab hold of that thing with your senses. Embrace some created thing with as many of the senses as you conveniently can do.

Be aware of it. The Word of God made flesh in Jesus of Nazareth is present in that thing, sustaining it in being.

See, the heavens do declare the glory of God, and the firmament does show forth his handiwork. Tonight you can go out and embrace a star, worship and adore the Word of God present in the spacious firmament on high. Sure. But you don't have to be nearly as grandiose as that. You can reach into your pocket and hold a piece of chewing gum. It, no less than the spacious firmament on high, declares the presence of the One who sustains it in being.

We live in a radically sacramental universe. I often think the presence of God is like when you cover your eyes with your hands, and it's not that your hands aren't there, it's just that they're too close. God has impregnated himself in his creation. It's the divine closeness that's the problem, not the divine absence. We have to back off from it in order to see it. You see what I mean about focusing your prayer?

OK, so Jesus is present in created things. He's also present in people. Now if he's present in other people in exactly the same way he's present in creation, in that he's got the whole world in his hands, he's got you.

If the eternal Word of God made flesh in Jesus stopped loving you on the count of three, you would go up in a puff of smoke. He's holding you in being;

he's caressing you with a divine dynamism just as he is your chair or your pencil. But with us, it's even more. For the eternal Word of God, which is the express image of the Father, is sustaining us in being not just as some thing, but as the image of God.

Wherever there is a human being, there is the image of God. That's why we are so infinitely precious. In the room where you are right now, if you could see them, are Elijah and Elisha. We don't see the angelic hosts; by definition, they're invisible, we can't see them. But they look at us and they surround us with amazement because we are in the image, male and female. Do you want to adore the power and presence of God? Do you want to touch God? Do you want to touch the holy? Just reach out, it's all around you.

That same old funny English bishop, when he found out that I had had some elementary experience of the presence of God, gave me some exercises. He said, "Bob, I want you to go ride the subway. I want you to sit there and with your eyes go around the subway car. And I want you to look at everybody, and I want you to celebrate the presence of God by saying, 'Jesus in you bless me, Jesus in you bless me.'"

Do you see the reality of it? The image is there, being sustained in being there. You say, "But, maybe that person's a drunk. Maybe that person's not a good person, maybe that person is one of 'them,' whoever 'them' is."

And the answer is, "hush, hush, hush." We never see Jesus in his human creation except as he is crucified by our sins. He's always there. Even when he's crucified by our sins, the image blesses. I call out to Jesus in the other person and ask the Jesus in the other person to bless me. And it works the other way, because after I've gone around the whole subway car invoking the blessing of Jesus, then I can say, "Jesus in me, bless you."

Do you think a society as violent as ours could stand some devotional exercises like that? Do you think that a society as racially hateful as ours could stand some praying like that?

In all the world there is nothing holier than another human being, for he or she is the place where God dwells. That's what makes our sin so dreadful. That's what makes our racism so blasphemous. That's what makes our addictions so awful, because we have to blaspheme and trash the temples.

Then, realize that Jesus is present not only in things, not only in other people but also—and this will bring tears to your eyes—he is present in you. And present not only in creation, although that is screamingly, exquisitely beautiful; not only in the image, although that tears the mind and heart to conceive of it; he tabernacles in us not only through creation and image, but also through baptism and Eucharist. The risen Christ dwells in us. Immediately you will start with your "buts." "But, but, but… But I'm not worthy. But I'm such a sinner. But there's not a promise or vow I've not betrayed in thought or word or deed, but, but, but…"

And he says, "Peace. My presence in you is not a function of your worthiness. It is the direct consequence of my love. Yes, you don't deserve it. Yes, I will it."

The center of your being is where Jesus dwells. Now, this is where the Jesus Prayer really comes home, when we address it to the "Lord Jesus Christ, Son of God," and he's right there. Turn to the Lord, drawing down the attention of the mind into the heart and call upon him there.

If he—by whom all things were made, he—who for us and our salvation came down from heaven, and was incarnate by the Holy Ghost of the Virgin Mary, he—who in the night in which he was betrayed took bread and when he had given thanks broke it and said, "This is my body" and with the cup "This is my blood," he—who in baptism made us sharers of his risen life, and he—who Sunday by Sunday feeds us with his most precious body and blood—is joined with us, it will never, never, never be sundered.

Is this all just a pretty dream? No, it's what the doctrine of creation is all about. He sustained all things with the word of his might. He creates us in his image, and in baptism and Eucharist we become that beautiful thing that St. Paul says—"in Christo."

You know, to be a Christian is not to be a good person. I am a Christian, and I am not a good person. I am not even very nice sometimes. I will now whisper a horrible truth into your ear: by yourself, you are not good, either, and you are not nice sometimes. We are all inheritors of a fallen nature.

Good and nice are not worth debate. The only thing that's worth diddly, and it's worth every diddly, is that we are new and that we dwell in him and he in us. To be a Christian is to be a sharer of the life of Christ. It's to be "in Christo," in Christ. It's to be able to be a living sacrament of his presence in our world and in our environment. It's to be able to bless; it's to be able to take the fabric of creation, the bread and the wine, and all of the bread and the wine— the bread and the wine of your house and your job, of your workplace, and bless it and break it and say, "This is part of the body of Christ." That's what being a Christian is. Never mind all that heaven stuff. It's to be able to grab the bread and the wine of creation and to make it new. To be able to embrace other people and say, "Forgiveness is real, blessing is real." Go down inside and say the Jesus Prayer there to him, there. If you want to say it out loud, do it. Lip movements I would recommend. Nobody's watching.

O Almighty God, you pour out on all who desire it the spirit of grace and supplication: Deliver us, when we draw near to you, from coldness of heart and wanderings of mind, that with steadfast thoughts and kindled affections we may worship you in spirit and in truth; through Jesus Christ Our Lord. Amen. (BCP, 1979, p. 833)

**Lord Jesus Christ, Son of God,
Have mercy on me, a sinner. Amen.**

Personal Reflection

How have you come to know the Presence of Jesus in you?

In others? In the creation? In human community?

Chapter Six

LIVING WITH THE JESUS PRAYER

The first consequence of knowing the Jesus Prayer is this: if anything is to come of it, it will depend in large part upon you—the extent to which you try to do your own exploring with the Jesus Prayer. Apart from that, knowing the Jesus Prayer will remain simply an interesting and inspirational experience but without any real subsequent impact. I hope you have some kind of rule of life, that there is something you do about morning prayer, something you do about evening prayer, that you participate regularly in the Eucharist, and all of those kinds of things. What I would suggest—and this is very concrete— very practical advice—is that you take something like 10 minutes a day for starters, and say, "For the next three months, the next 90 days, I'm going to try to bring my mind down into my heart and pray the Jesus Prayer to Christ living within me." The amount of time is not so important as it is that there be some commitment to some time. Certainly, you do not want to be extravagant and say you'll do it for five hours a day, because you won't. But what is important is a fixed, forced, deliberate, intentional saying of the prayer orally—with the lips, the tongue, and everything. That will get you started, and then after a generous commitment of something like three months, you will know what you want to do next. You might want to continue, you might want to increase, or you may say, "Thanks, but no thanks." All of those responses are fine.

The second consequence of knowing the Jesus Prayer is that it is a powerful aid to the development of what traditional spirituality calls habitual recollection. What the tradition means by recollection is living in the presence of God. Habitual recollection means that one consciously lives in the presence of God habitually. Every spiritual writer that I know of really does think that this is tremendously important. It is my belief that anyone who is a priest, a pastor, or a spiritual director should know about habitual recollection, or be practicing habitual recollection. One of the things that you will want to do is to move along toward that state of habitual recollection, living in the presence of God.

Now, interestingly enough, there is in our midst, by the mighty operation of the Holy Spirit, a lovely secular spirituality which bubbled up or was let down from heaven in the early decades of the last century. It is the spirituality of the 12 Steps. The community in which the 12-step spirituality emerged was the community of Alcoholics Anonymous, and there is a connection between the 12 Steps and traditional Christian spirituality. Not everybody's immediately aware of it, but it's there.

The original hospitality that enabled AA to begin was an Oxford Group home associated with Frank Beckmann's Oxford Group Movement in Ohio. But a connection with classical Christian spirituality did not so much come from there as it came from two priests who were friends and, indeed, spiritual directors to Bill Wilson, the founder of AA. One of them was a Jesuit and the other was an Episcopalian named Sam Shoemaker. What happened in AA, and I like to use this word because I think it is appropriate for AA, was a distillation of some really fundamentally profound Christian ascetical principles. You can just run through those 12 Steps, and at every point, they will make contact with the great tradition of classical Christian spirituality. One of the steps, referred to as the mainentance part of the 12-step program, talks about conscious contact with God. That's the point at which the classical language of habitual recollection intersects with conscious contact. What is happening in that intersection is an awareness that all subsequent growing presupposes conscious contact, presupposes habitual recollection.

I knew a wonderful abbot at the Pecos Benedictine Abbey who, almost without exception, when someone came to him for spiritual direction, handed them a prayer rope and a copy of the Jesus Prayer. That was an acknowledgment that no matter where you are in the spiritual life, the quickest way to move ahead is to begin to live a life of habitual recollection, living in the presence of God.

There is a wonderful old hymn that says, "He walks with me and He talks with me and He tells me I am His own." When you use that language, a lot of good things are going to happen. There are a lot of people who are terribly lonely and terribly frightened and sort of profoundly interiorized. One of the ways to handle that profound interiorization is to begin to realize in a concrete and spiritually practical way that you aren't alone. You are the beloved of God. That is what habitual recollection will do; it is what continuous contact will do.

It seems to me that our culture is obsessively compulsive. We have turned obsessive compulsion into an art form. It is not the great classical addictions that drive us, but all kinds of obsessive compulsions. I don't know how many homes I go into to take someone the Eucharist where the first thing I want to say is, "For God's sake we are about to make our communions; would you please turn the television off." It goes, and it goes, and it goes, and it goes. We become addicted to that electronic stimulation. We're addicted to diversions and to distraction. That's why it is so hard for contemporary people to meditate, because they have become addicted to distraction. If you move away the distraction, they become exceedingly uncomfortable. With any luck at all, we are rapidly approaching, as adults, the attention span of a five-year-old. For all of this contemporary, really quite profound spiritual malaise, habitual recollection is very important. I am not interested in the Jesus Prayer so much from the standpoint of the study of some arcane, ancient Russian Orthodox technique, as I think it is the mother lode for making some important headway in a very real contemporary problem.

Another thing about the Jesus Prayer is that it is a powerful assist in growing toward and growing in contemplative prayer. You may be familiar with the different labels of prayer: liturgical prayer, intercessory prayer, and petitionary prayer. There are all of those kinds of praying, and then there is meditation. Usually in the Western Church when we talk about meditation, we are talking about the use of the imagination—picturing Jesus in a boat. For a lot of people, this is a very rewarding pattern of prayer. You may be familiar with *Day by Day,* or in the Methodist tradition *The Upper Room,* or any of the other daily readings. Each of those is intended to be a triggering device to get the imagination flowing. And they're all fine publications. Ultimately, however, the point of all meditation and imaging is to come into the presence of God and there to be in adoration and love, participating in the divine embrace. It's the wordless, imageless, "I love you—you love me."

Growing in the Jesus Prayer is a splendid resource for growing in contemplation. With the Jesus Prayer, you are ready to contemplate while you wash the dishes, while you walk the dog, while you clean the ring out of the toilet bowl. Once that small murmuring stream is there, even if it goes under the surface of consciousness for a little bit, it will bubble up again.

The Jesus Prayer becomes something that you can let flow and flow without giving it your full attention. For instance, when I am in a counseling situation with someone, I give that person my full conscious contact, but even while I am thus engaged, the "Lord Jesus Christ, have mercy on me, a sinner," is flowing along. And it doesn't diminish attention; it doesn't diminish perception; it heightens it. Because ultimately you don't want to come to Bob Hibbs, because Bob Hibbs will mess you up every time all by himself. You need better resources than Bob Hibbs has got. You need the one who dwells within Bob Hibbs. You don't have to be a priest or a spiritual director to constantly come into contact with people who need the one who dwells within you.

Here's another way to use the Jesus Prayer. Do you like to go to church and just be in that holy place? What do you do when you go into the church? What do you do when you focus on the cross? Or on the Blessed Sacrament reserved in the tabernacle? Well, "Lord Jesus Christ, Son of God" is a delightful and wonderful and strengthening way to spend that time in the sacred place.

OK, let's talk about temptation. Temptation is dreadful. It is also an inevitable part of being a Christian. I am a patsy for temptation. I never met a temptation I didn't like, and most of them I've yielded to.

But Jesus was tempted, and I know of no way to be a Christian that does not involve temptation. It's part of the given of being baptized. I think it is part of the given of being created.

Sometimes there is no mental defense against temptation. I have a friend who has been a member of Alcoholics Anonymous for 15 years, and he told me this story. Some time ago, after he had been sober for many years, his wife asked him to stop by a barbecue place one evening to pick up some barbecue to take home for dinner. As he waited for the barbecue to be sliced, a nice young lady said to him, "Wouldn't you like to wait in the bar?" And there it was, he told me—temptation. Wouldn't it be nice just to have one little drink in that quiet little bar where no one knew him…

Lord Jesus Christ, Son of God, have mercy on me a sinner.

There are times—there is no other way to put this—that we are assaulted by our ancient enemy. The shield and sword of the Jesus Prayer is a mighty, mighty resource at those times.

There are times when temptation is not that sudden confrontation but is a subtle enchantment, a delicate play between the intellect and the will. The intellect presents something to the will and it looks attractive and the will inclines toward it. And then the intellect presents the means to the end and the will inclines toward it. Then the intellect presents the means as obtainable and the will inclines toward it. Gradually every intellectual defense is eroded away, and the next thing you know you are in the embrace of the enemy.

If the minute that stinking process begins, I flee to the Jesus Prayer and trust the one who lives in me, it doesn't happen.

So that it is not a total loss, it helps to remember that temptation is the anvil on which our sanctity is hammered out. It's just that some of us are very slow learners.

There is another temptation that is offered to us today. Thirty years ago, when I was first ordained priest, you couldn't find anybody who wanted to talk about spirituality. There were a couple of relatively old-fashioned seminaries in the Episcopal Church at the time, and thank God, I went to one of them. There, we talked about priests as physicians of souls. At the time, it all sounded dreadfully quaint, medieval, and arcane. Everybody else was doing psychology, psychology, psychology.

But in the years since then, spirituality has taken off like a rocket. Today it's a growth industry. Everyone who's anyone has been to a retreat, and books and tapes proliferate. All of this is good, with one notable exception, and that is the degree to which a lot of Christian spirituality has tended to become sort of Gnostic navel gazing. It becomes the flight of the alone to be alone. It becomes a kind of privatized me and God, me and Jesus. And that's not good, that's not Christian. It is pretty good Buddhism, it is excellent Neoplatonism, but it's not incarnational Christianity.

Some years ago, when I was working out at the gym a lot, I discovered that some people are attracted to the gym so that they can look in a mirror and sort of study their own musculature. There is a part of our contemporary enthusiasm for spirituality that reminds me of that; it has a narcissistic quality about it: I want to be holy because holy is what I want to be. Or, I want to be in the presence of God because living in the presence of God makes me feel good.

Jesus tells us what's wrong with cultivating spiritual muscles for the sake of cultivating spiritual muscles. We are, after all, part of the body of Christ. We are a continuation of the incarnation in time, and it is our apostolic ministry to be Christ in our environments. We are the salt of the earth, we are light, we are life. The image that I find very helpful is that we are the food for the world. I think the Eucharist is a wonderful model. I think it is not for nothing that the Eucharist is the center and the heart of the worship of the Christian community. Not so that week by week we can go get our batteries charged, but so that week by week we may discover yet one more time who we are. We are the body of Christ, we are the blood of Christ, we are the life of Christ given for the life of the world.

We are the bread he takes into his holy and venerable hands; we are the wine that he takes into his holy and venerable hands. He blesses us, he breaks us, and he says of us, "You are my body, you are my blood. Now go on, get out of here, and feed the world, die and rise, die and rise. That in you and through you and in me through you, the world may live."

I think that's all true and it scares the britches off of me. Because I'm chicken, I am afraid to die. I am afraid to risk. I love Episcopalians, but Episcopalians do not, in general, take great risks for Jesus. An Episcopalian thinks he is being an evangelist when he puts a lovely little "Welcome to the Episcopal Church" bumper sticker on the back of his car.

Yet, in and through the Jesus Prayer, I am learning that I am not alone. Things that I could not do by myself and do not do by myself, someone else can do in me and through me.

You may know that slogan "One with Christ is a majority." That is a nice idea, but we really don't know what it means until we understand that He dwells in us. And we in him. He is our strength, he is our power, he is our courage, and in him and with him and by him, in the unity of the Holy Spirit, we

can go out into the world and take its bread and its
wine and make them what he has made us to be:
His body, His blood, and His life.

*Lord make us instruments of your peace. Where there
is hatred let us sow love; where there is injury, pardon;
where there is discord, union; where there is doubt, faith;
where there is despair, hope; where there is darkness,
light; where there is sadness, joy. Grant that we may not
so much seek to be consoled as to console, to be understood as to understand, to be loved as to love, for it is
in giving that we receive, it is in pardoning that we are
pardoned, and it is in dying that we are born to eternal
life. Amen.* (BCP, 1979, p. 833)

**Lord, Jesus Christ, Son of God,
Have mercy on me, a sinner. Amen.**

Personal Reflection

How have you experienced temptation?

*What guidance does the Jesus Prayer offer when
temptation comes?*

About the Author

Following graduation from General Theological Seminary in 1957, The Rt. Rev. Robert B. Hibbs began his ministry in Toronto, Ontario while pursuing his graduate work. For fifteen years, he was on the faculty of St. Andrew's Theological Seminary, Quezon City, Philippines where he served as a faculty member, Sub-Dean and later Dean. Later, he also served on the faculty of the Seminary of the Southwest, Austin, Texas. For five years Bishop Hibbs served in the Diocese of Northwest Texas as Vicar of St. Peter's, Borger, then Vicar/Rector of St. Stephen's, Lubbock. In 1988, he finally arrived in the Diocese of West Texas, serving first at St. Barnabas', Fredericksburg, as Rector, then at the Church of the Good Shepherd Corpus Christi, as Assistant Rector. As Bishop Suffragan, his particular passions included Recovery Ministries, both in the diocese and with the National Church, and the Cursillo Movement.

Upon retirement as Bishop Suffragan, it was his joy to spend hours reading, listening to classical music and cheering on the Missions baseball team. He was active as a member of the Texas Coalition to Abolish the Death Penalty. In addition, his gift of listening encouraged many to regard him as a mentor and spiritual director.

Bob Hibbs, retired Bishop Suffragan of the Episcopal Diocese of West Texas, died in April 2017 in San Antonio.

How it all Began

This lovely book, *An Altar in Your Heart* by Bob Hibbs, began as a two-day retreat organized by Jennifer and Charles Garrett of Stillpoint Media. They recognized that Bob Hibbs' retreat on the Jesus Prayer could become a book that would bless those who were not present for the retreat. Jennifer and Charles have been instrumental in helping shape the 20th Anniversary Edition. It was they that suggested with the family's approval that Material Media include the CD with the excerpts from the retreat.

For those who wish to hear the entire retreat and Bob's resonant, stirring voice, the audio version of the original retreat is available. You may download it for $9.99 on MateralMedia.com or purchase a set of 5 CDs for $20 (including domestic shipping) from MaterialMedia.com or StillpointMedia.com. You then will be able to experience not only his voice but also his humor and wisdom.

The questions at the end of each chapter also make this book an ideal 6-week study course. Classes or personal study can benefit from the retreat audio.

The Retreat
The Jesus Prayer Retreat
Downloadable Audio: 978-1-94746-01-0
CD set (Audio Disc): 978-1-94746002-7

The Book
An Altar in Your Heart
Print: ISBN 978-0-9967535-9-3
E-book: ISBN 978-1-947460-00-3

About the Artist

Luc Freymanc is a German-born, U.S.-based artist who publishes under his pen-name a very large and still growing series of drawings of Jesus Christ. He sees his work in the tradition of German expressionism. Most of his drawings are about the passion of Christ, intended to remind the viewer of the demands of the Christian faith.

For more information: www.Freymanc.com

20th Anniversary Edition Acknowledgments

It has been a pleasure to work with and meet Bob Hibbs' family—David, Lisa and his beloved wife Nancy—to publish a new edition of *An Altar in Your Heart: Meditations on the Jesus Prayer.*

Thanks also to the Garretts, especially Jennifer for her excellent suggestion to include reflection questions. Additional thanks are due to Eleanor Stomberger, Marjorie George, Laura Shaver, and to The Rev. Mary C. Earle for her insightful foreword and for help with the reflection questions.

Each chapter is graced with a meditative ink wash by Luc Freymanc who generously gave his blessing.

The beautiful layout and cover design are the work of Andréa Caillouet—artist, designer and friend. Thank you.

An Altar in Your Heart: Meditations on the Jesus Prayer is a celebration of Bob's vast and varied ministry. His humor, his understanding of people, his commitment to honesty, and his sound theology made him a beloved teacher, pastor, and friend.

We hope this book introduces a new audience to "The Jesus Prayer" and calls others back to this ancient and beautiful prayer.

Elizabeth Cauthorn
Jennifer Jutz
Material Media LLC

Praise for the Book

For those of us who sometimes become frantic and despairing in our quest for a richer, deeper (and perhaps more elaborate) prayer life, the ancient Jesus Prayer is like a cup of cool water on an August afternoon— refreshing, reassuring, calming. From the heart and lips of Bishop Bob Hibbs, the Prayer enlarges into a spring-fed pool, inviting us to take the plunge.

Those who were blessed by the life and ministries of Bishop Hibbs will be delighted to hear again his voice in these meditations. Twenty years later, the grace, humility, wisdom and playfulness still shine through. And to those finding this book—or the Jesus Prayer—for the first time: Come on in; the water's fine.

The Right Rev. David Reed
Bishop of the Diocese of West Texas

Perhaps the greatest sickness of modern Christianity is a faith that is a mile wide and a quarter inch deep. This little book, this reflection on the Jesus prayer, offers us the antidote for that illness. Bob Hibbs was a living saint who walked among us disguised as a bishop, spreading wisdom and kindness and laughter and love wherever he went. We could all use more of that.

James R. Dennis, O.P.
Author of *Correspondence in D Minor*